How to Turn Your
Small Business into a
"Category of One"

How to Turn Your Small Business into a "Category of One"

Before You Spend Another Dime on Traditional Advertising!

Dan Persigehl

Copyright © 2018 by Dan Persigehl.

Library of Congress Control Number:		2018908726
ISBN:	Hardcover	978-1-9845-4270-0
	Softcover	978-1-9845-4269-4
	eBook	978-1-9845-4268-7

All rights reserved. No part of this book may be reproduced or transmitted in any form or by any means, electronic or mechanical, including photocopying, recording, or by any information storage and retrieval system, without permission in writing from the copyright owner.

The views expressed in this work are solely those of the author and do not necessarily reflect the views of the publisher, and the publisher hereby disclaims any responsibility for them.

Any people depicted in stock imagery provided by Getty Images are models, and such images are being used for illustrative purposes only. Certain stock imagery © Getty Images.

Print information available on the last page.

Rev. date: 08/09/2018

To order additional copies of this book, contact:
Xlibris
1-888-795-4274
www.Xlibris.com
Orders@Xlibris.com
781553

How to turn your small business into a "Category of ONE"... Before you spend another dime on advertising!

Why I wrote this book...

I battle a powerful addiction... Efficient, affordable and effective Marketing and Messaging. Small business and professional services advertising should be an investment, not an expense. I spent 27 years in creative media, mostly radio, and over those years I saw literally millions of dollars being wasted for a variety of specific reasons. The 2 most common flaws are a lack of strategic preparation, and the messaging didn't activate their target consumer. But there many more.

In most cases they simply weren't ready to advertise their product or service, and no one there prevented them from the dreaded **"Advertising victim"** syndrome. They simply reacted emotionally before planning strategically. Two years ago I discovered several common sense fundamentals that caught my eye. So much so that I spent more than a year researching every piece of this unique source of actionable information as I could. I was fortunate to find much more than I anticipated and it inspired me to use it as a foundation for my leap into the entrepreneurial galaxy and launch DP Media Consultants. I launched a website at www.killermessaging.com to offer content marketing and messaging help to small businesses and start-ups with limited budgets. There are ad agencies and consultants abound to help those businesses with huge budgets, but very few that focus on those who need the most help. It's just not profitable enough for these greedy entities. I'll give what I hope is proper credit and attribution to the man responsible for these incredible concepts in the final chapter of this book. Proper, but not as deserving as warranted as you'll see if you're kind enough to read on.

Now, let me be clear, I also witnessed wildly successful advertising campaigns and I spotlight some of those in this book. This is because 99% of small business advertisers only deal with their media rep from start to failure. This really began in 1996 when President Clinton signed the telecommunications act. This when the big media conglomerates came together and went public. The single most important strategy became cutting expenses. Entire departments were eliminated. The reality of this is it's the same strategy today. Frankly, you'd need to hire a private detective to find a radio station with an actual creative department today. In most cases small business advertisers count on the untrained media rep to handle the copywriting, production and placement. Media reps are compensated only by the revenue they bring in, up front.

Find me a media company today that compensates their reps based on the success of the campaign or, results. They are instructed to "do what it takes to get the business". Don't blame the media reps for this, this problem began when media companies started downsizing their staffs to cut expenses and please their investors on Wall street. Media reps these days have so much pressure on them to generate revenue they simply can't, and don't take the time and strategic planning it takes to put together a truly successful campaign. The bottom line is, most media companies and ad agencies don't care if your campaign succeeds or not. Just keep churning that new business! Don't believe me? I'm married to a media rep. Her bonus compensation is based on how much NEW business she brings in. There is no bonus compensation for re-upping clients. Yet the adage that "80% of your business comes from 20% of your clients" doesn't seem to apply to most traditional agency and media companies. Still trust that kind of policy and mindset to generate your messaging?

Full disclosure, as Regional Creative Director and National Creative team member with multiple major media companies, I was actually forced to participate in many campaigns that I knew were dead on arrival. "Just do what the customer wants!" was the mantra. I begged several of my Sales Managers to have just one of their weekly meetings focused on creatively unique, successful campaigns, and why they were successful? It never happened.

I decided that someone, other than expensive ad agencies that many small businesses can't afford, needs to help small business advertisers start getting consistent **results** from the beginning. Help them become a **"Category of ONE."** To help them prepare to advertise. What does "prepare to advertise" mean? That's what this book is all about. Warning! This requires collaboration with the advertiser, and a willingness in some cases, to change their marketing strategy. Some advertisers are simply too stubborn and unwilling to commit to the process. Those are the folks who likely have bad experiences with their advertising and blame the media rep and/or the media platform(s) they used. Rarely is the messaging blamed for failure, yet at least 90% of the time weak, irrelevant messaging is indeed the cause. Ego can be a powerful thing. Messaging is the first place to start when the advertising isn't working. Small businesses and startups need a partner who is affordable, efficient and effective. The competition for consumer's attention gets tougher every day. Just to be clear, I'm no longer looking to work with the major national advertisers I've worked with in the past like Pepsi, Geico or Home Depot. I want to offer a service that provides solid strategy, killer messaging and a professionally vested partnership at a price any small business can afford. I am on a mission to help as many small businesses as I can become a **"Category of ONE"**.

What area can you DOMINATE?

Don't go any further into your quest to DOMINATE until you can clearly say it, prove it and share it! Go ahead, you've come this far. Whoever made up the phrase... "Competition makes us all better" is a moron who's never owned a small business. If the #1 reason you're in business is to make as much money as possible, read no further. There's no "cum by ya" here. Crushing your competitors makes you more money! So, what can your small business DOMINATE in your competitive environment? Start with determining where your competitors are most vulnerable. Then decide if it makes sense to reference in your headline, **Point of Differentiation** or just a part of your body of content. It doesn't matter if a competitor is already doing something similar, you're going to do it in a whole new way. What is the primary strength or benefit your competitors have? Don't be afraid to turn that around and use it against them. **You can't half-ass this!** You've got to have a BAD-ASS mindset! Domination is hard. It requires supreme focus. It can require long hours. It requires that you be prepared to give up some things you've enjoyed for a long time. But it's so worth it! Let's break it down...

#1 Is there a specific area in your business category that is currently being under-served or poorly served?

#2 Who do you consider to be your primary competition in your category? What are their strengths? Where are they the most vulnerable?

#3 Understand that ideas create thought.... Solutions create evangelists!

#4 Are you willing to **attack yourself** once a quarter?

#5 Do you understand your message is **never delivered from a "ain't we neat"** perspective. Your messaging will **always be about how your business will impact your customer's lives.** It's not about you or your business (this is sometimes the hardest aspect for some to grasp)?

#6 Are you willing to utilize **Contrarian Thinking** to **disrupt** your industry?

#7 Are you willing to consider non-traditional strategies, message placement points and personalization (more on this later...)?

#8 Are you committed to **only** use media platforms that are easily measured?

#9 Do you have a rock-solid **referral** plan in place?

#10 Do you understand that the ultimate goal is to have customers **search for you**?

I'll explain these in greater detail and share some success stories later in the book.

Captivate, Motivate and Activate!

Your messaging should meet the "**Successful messaging trifecta**", which is captivate, motivate and activate your target consumer group. Anything less is a waste of marketing time and resources. Here's how it's done...

Captivate

Do not waste time with trivial intros. You have **5 seconds** to captivate consumers with your messaging. There are simply too many distractions and messages consumers are flooded with daily. Your first 5 seconds, on any platform is your **headline.** Let me share some examples of winners and losers from actual advertising campaigns... Imagine you're on your daily commute and you see or hear the following small business advertising headlines... How would you react, if at all?

Losers-

"At Mason auto repair, we're your local, family owned repair facility for over 50 years!" (who cares? see Walmart...)

"It's the sale you've been waiting for!" (REALLY?! How the hell do you know what I'm thinking? **Never use assumptive messaging!**)

"Hi! I'm Duke Boring, general manager at Duke's Autoplex!

(you lost me at Hi!)

Compare those headlines to these headlines...

Winners-

"Imagine... lounging in your padded beach chair with the magestic ocean purring just feet away..."

"I never dreamed I could lose 60 pounds in 6 months without some kind of gastric or cosmetic surgery, but I did!"

"That little fella is just a few feet away from becoming a tragic loss that you may never get over"

I hope the fundamental differences in those winners and losers is obvious to you. Notice that the winner's headlines focus on an emotional benefit that makes has an immediate impact on the consumers lives? They can immediately see themselves in the scenario you've created. You've captivated their mind.

Notice that the loser's headlines completely focus on **their** business? If your message headline doesn't emotionally captivate any particular consumer group, it's a LOSER!

To captivate any target consumer group you must **cut to the chase!** The first question your messaging must answer is "What's in it for me?" Your message headline must evoke an emotional reaction. The two most powerful emotions consumers feel are... a fear of loss and how do I gain from this? In your messaging you need to include "why?" What motivated you to do business as you are? "Why" is much more meaningful content than who, what, where and how (though you need to answer all of these at some point, just not in your headline) "Why?" triggers emotion. The others are simply information you hope consumers retain.

Motivate

In order for your small business to motivate consumers, you must first identify their primary challenge you intend to overcome, followed by your solution. If you're clearly the "new kid on the block" in your industry, include comparisons to the big, greedy competitor in your way. Turn their advertised benefit against them in your headline message. Unless there is such a significant difference in pricing, stay away from pricing comparisons. In small business marketing, pricing is the easiest attribute to squash, especially if your competitor has more marketing resources than you. If your message is rooted in low prices, your message will sound just like every auto dealer or grocery store campaign, except for the auto dealer I worked with in Portland, Oregon. (I'll share the story in detail a bit later)

Comparisons should be based on a benefit your competitor either can't or won't challenge. But 99 times out of 100, the difference should be in the unmatched personal service and/or the unique experience the consumer will appreciate when they do business with you. Make them "feel something" when they hear or see your campaign. Consumers aren't dumb! They have access to more information than they'll ever need these days, and they use it. Motivation is affirmation! If a consumer is motivated to learn more about your Primary Point of Differentiation they heard or saw in your messaging, they will likely visit your website and your social media posts (more on this later...). On average, consumers visit your website/social media at least 3 times before making a buying decision. You must identify the challenge and your solution on every media platform you utilize. Be everywhere your target consumers are. Keep the consumer emotionally engaged no matter where or how many times they visit your website and social media. Motivation is affirmation!

Activate

Activation occurs when you've made an emotional connection. You've got their attention with your message headline. You've clearly identified the challenge and you've told them how your small business can help them overcome that challenge. Now you need to show or tell them the specific, compelling value they'll get when they choose to do business with you instead of your competitor. It's time to share your irresistible offer that makes them feel good about doing business with you, and a deadline to take advantage of it. You can always use the often used "due to amazing response from our original offer, we've decided to extend it..." Activation means the customer has invited you into their space. Activation means they no longer need to Google search your industry. Activation means they can't resist your offer. They want to learn more! Activation means they are giving you the chance to close the deal! Unless you're a one-person show, this means you need a well-trained staff that can answer most any question a consumer asks. You need a receptionist or customer service rep to be the perfect ambassador for your business. You could even tie that benefit back to your Primary Point of Differentiation... "we'll make your buying/expert search experience quicker and smarter because we have the best trained staff in the industry that won't waste your time..." One more thing to remember... for God's sake NEVER make a consumer wait more than 2 minutes after they enter your business before you engage them or offer to answer any questions they might have. Make it clear that your favorite part of the relationship is answering questions. Put reading materials in your lobby that they won't see at any competitor. If you're in the professional services sector where appointments are needed, don't put magazines focused on your industry on the lobby table. Have a wide variety of pop culture, marketing, financial and even pet magazines right in front of them. Boredom kills opportunity before you even get the chance to meet the customer. Offer something of entertainment value to them and their mood will be naturally enhanced. Make the actual appointment seem like a disruption to their visit. Trivial as it may seem, this is an opportunity to be a **"Category of ONE"** before any service or transaction has taken place. The key is to keep your value proposition simple and easy to share. When executed properly, there is a wonderful, dual benefit for your business... it's your opportunity to close the deal AND get referrals! It gets better... The ultimate goal is to build that consumer relationship and activate them to join your loyalty rewards program. The next step is to keep that customer engaged consistently with relevant content across your media platforms and conversation. New customers are like that beautiful houseplant you need to water every couple days or it will begin to shrivel up and go away. Customer attrition can be significantly reduced IF you keep them consistently engaged with relevant content after closing the initial deal. **Don't half-ass this!**

Is your website mobile friendly?

It better be. This is the single most important "must have" element for your small business website. Hubspot.com recently concluded an extensive study on search devices and found that almost 80% of all web searches take place on a mobile device, and that number will continue to rise. Is your website really easy to navigate on mobile devices? Though I would never recommend or encourage this activity, your website needs to offer all the information consumers want and need within the time they spend sitting at a stoplight. Test this yourself or better yet, have people you know and trust test it for you. It doesn't matter how visually, over the top graphics or dynamic content you have if the consumer has to scroll down too far to get the most important message information they need. By all means fill your website with compelling content including colorful graphics, photos, even testimonials and storytelling they can scroll down to see… just don't make it the first thing consumers see when they have less than a minute before that left-turn signal turns green. Your website needs to captivate, motivate and activate in 2 minutes or less viewing time. **Don't half-ass this!**

Be "Socially Responsible"

Successful small business marketing is primarily rooted in getting your unique, compelling message to as many potential customers as possible when they are most likely to make a decision to do business with you or a competitor. This is critical... You need to be where potential customers are. I am a strong believer that you should use a minimum of 2 social media platforms to drive engagement and web hits. My favorites for small business are You tube, twitter, facebook and instagram. These platforms are unique and require a style that best fits the platform. You can't just cut and paste content on every platform. Each platform has some unique rules and guidelines you need to be aware of. You need to focus on presenting content that is "native" to every platform used. Put any personal conflicts you may have with social media aside. Again, your messaging isn't about you, it's about captivating, motivating and activating your target consumer group. I've actually had initial client meetings where the client simply refused to utilize social media for personal reasons. YOUR MESSAGING ISN'T ABOUT YOU! Keep personal opinions out of it! You are only limiting your success if you refuse to go where your potential customers/clients are. Yes, I politely thanked these folks for their time and left. I use an online service called "social examiner" to stay on top of trendsetting concepts and execution in social media. I utilize their concepts with every client I work with as part of my service.

But, keep your social media posts about your customers. Stay away from negative, personal comments about most anything or anyone. It's petty and unnecessary. Share customer/client success stories or unique challenges you tackled with them... Be the social media site your target consumer group goes to feel good about real people, especially you. Don't present your small business like the clergyman who uses social media as a pulpit to constantly post about "condemnation" and personal issues with his church. Something he or she would never do during a church service. Be consistent, yet dynamic in social messaging and reinforce your Primary Point of Differentiation.

Timing is also a critical part of your small business social media impact. You should always post near the time your target consumer group is likely to make a decision that might lead to commerce for your business. For example, if you're an Orthodontist, post right before school or in the early evening when parents have the time to notice your post, discuss it and make decisions. If you're a retail store, post right before drivetimes, including lunchtime. Use common sense. Don't overthink this. Keep an "outside/in" mindset. Research the time of day your customers likely search and decide. In other words, always think like your target consumer group and focus your messaging the same way.

Would you post about your kid's lemonade stand at night? I hope not, if you want the maximum benefit. The most important reason social media posting needs to be timely is, if you post at the wrong time your post may be buried way down the list and you've likely handed the consumers you are after over to your competitor. People are lazy by nature... they don't search very long or hard to find an option post that addresses exactly what they're searching for. Always tie postings back to your Primary Point of Differentiation in both direct and in-direct ways. By the way, it's commonly a good idea to hire a social media expert that understands the fundamentals for success and knows how to tailor your message to the largest active social media audience available at the most opportune time. If you're a start-up or fairly new business that doesn't have decent cash flow yet, consider using college interns who are social media geeks. Google analytics is a fairly simple program to measure the success of your messaging... Social media posting is **FREE!** Yet it offers your small business a communication platform so abundant in potential leads and real-time customer feedback that even traditional media utilizes daily.

Topicality

Topicality offers a constant messaging and posting opportunity for your small business to piggyback on the big picture, trending topics the masses are already talking about. We all get "writers block" sometimes. We all have creative challenges to keep our content fresh and relevant. Topicality is the perfect remedy in these moments. One of my favorite exercises I use several times a week is writing down potential headlines that in some way tie back to my Primary point of Differentiation. Twitter's trending topics list is the perfect place to start. Be very careful about referencing internet website "news sites" for topicality, especially political subjects. Most of these news sites have agendas financed by political influencers, are not credible and can damage your credibility very quickly.

One area of topicality that too many small business social media posters have at their disposal, but fail to utilize, is their own lives. This makes you more tangible and relatable to potential customers. You'd be amazed at how much things you may perceive as mundane, are interesting to more people than you could imagine. These are tremendous posting threads generators. Consumers are on many occasions more interested in real stories from real people. It makes them feel like they are engaging with peers vs. propaganda. The more consumers know about you, even the embarrassing stuff, the more comfortable they are activating the buying process. Obscure holidays are another opportunity to post about. It just so happens that "National Diaper Day" postings are more likely to get shared than random, negative opinion postings. Use obscure holidays as unique marketing opportunities to build campaigns and postings around. Some examples of remarkable, fictitious potential campaigns from business categories you wouldn't expect to be associated with "National Diaper Day"...

Financial planner messaging-

"In honor of National Diaper Day, this week only, we're offering a safe investment that will insure and protect your child's college funding"

Walk-in pediatric clinic messaging-

"This week only, in association with National Diaper Day, we're giving away a free box of diapers with every check-up"

Personal injury attorney-

"National Diaper Day reminds us diapers prevent accidents. Some accidents can't be prevented. If you or someone you know has been injured in an accident and need cash until your case is settled, Browne & Associates will get you the cash you need to take care of your little ones in 24 hours or less!"

Build messaging around goofy holidays consistently multiple times every year and you'll enhance your core personality and build consumer anticipation. Curiosity is a great activator! One more important resource for effective messaging ideas is other industries. Study some of the most effective campaigns across all media and determine specifically what makes their message so effective... is it the creative?... is it the emotional draw?... is it simply outrageous?... How does it captivate, motivate and activate? There are simply too many advertisers who waste their valuable resources "copycatting" other advertiser campaigns in your own industry (Hello auto dealers!). Do you understand that copycatting and following the leader in your industry is lazy and ineffective? Understand that concepts that work in other industries can work in your industry and are perceived as original. YOU cannot afford to "play it safe". **Don't half-ass this!**

Direct response advertising is the most effective!

There are several reasons for this, but I'll start with the fact that direct response advertising can be accurately measured and held accountable. Traditional advertising (tv, radio, magazines...) is risky and a major part of traditional media rep training is learning how to handle objections.

Only use traditional media after you see evidence it's working on reviews and social media. Why is this? It's expensive, and largely unaccountable. Have you ever had a conversation with a traditional media rep where they took responsibility for the failed advertising campaign you just spent a fortune on, yet got little if any return on investment? Of course not, it's because they have no accountability. Direct response advertising is built on accountability.

If direct response marketing didn't work, our mailboxes wouldn't be filled with those over-sized postcards. When direct response marketing doesn't give the expected return it's almost always because it didn't even "captivate" the recipients. They are all the same size, use similar messaging and can easily be stacked into the "won't even look at it" pile and forgotten. Are you aware you can send your uniquely crafted Sales Letters in miniature garbage cans, poster tubes, wallets, oversize UPS or Fed-ex envelopes, coconut shells, popcorn bags... it's nearly limitless in scope.

To captivate customers you have to get their attention immediately. Make your packaging unavoidable!

When using traditional media your campaign time is limited so you need to drive home the "why", "how" and "where" to get the benefit multiple times in your campaign. Phone numbers and website URL's need to be mentioned at least 4 times in any media campaign, including 3 times in a row at the end of the message. The messaging strategy is significantly different on traditional media than Sales Letters or webinars. You simply need to make that critical emotional connection much quicker.

Sales Letter mailers also need to be personal. Refer to recipients by their first name on the front of the package and at the beginning of your Sales Letter. Believe it or not, handwritten campaigns work much better than slick, produced, thick-stock paper look alike campaigns. Believe it or not, legal pads work better than company stationary. There is an amazing company called **"Copydoodles"** that can print your messaging to make it look completely handwritten, with lines through misspelled words, underlining, arrows pointing to certain copy points, captions… anything that makes it real, and includes a sense of urgency. Check them out at **copydoodles.com**. Get out of your cocoon, spread your wings and let it fly! It's efficient, affordable and effective!

The most effective direct response campaigns are executed in 3 phases across multi-media platforms. The first campaign is always creative direct mail (captivation), then 2-3 weeks later it's followed up with a little more urgency and solutions in the message through a different media platform like email (motivation)… The third phase includes a hard-deadline to your offer and immediate, specific urgency like "you've only got 3 days to save" or "you'll kick yourself if you miss out on a deal like this!"(activation) Plus, you can track where every dollar is going and coming from. There are no excuses or rationalizing, just results, good or bad. Google analytics can give you a pretty good idea why your campaign failed. Feel free to reach out to me directly at dan@killermessaging.com if you want more details on how to effectively execute your direct response campaign. **Don't half-ass this!**

Utilize Content Marketing principles

Content Marketing is defined in what I consider the Content Marketing bible, "Content Marketing Works!" by Arnie & Brad Kuenn as...

***The art of providing relevant, valuable content to consumers without selling them anything or interrupting them.**

Instead of pitching your product or services, you deliver information that makes your prospects more informed before they buy.

If you deliver consistent, ongoing, valuable information to your prospects, they ultimately reward you with their business and loyalty.

Amen! Be a giver, not an unnecessary risk taker long before you advertise on traditional media (I refer to it as "cross your fingers advertising"). What makes Content

Marketing a **"Category of ONE"** is there is no finish line. It should be a permanent strategy designed to consistently captivate, motivate and activate prospects.

Content marketing is the best tool out there to build "expert" status and trust in your industry, 2 perceptions that draw new business that desires long term relationships. The goal is to make your small business a "go-to source" for information in your industry, as well as the "go-to source" for products and/or services. This is how your evangelists are cultivated. The key to successful Content marketing is taking the time needed to study your target consumer group in advance. What kind of information are they commonly searching for? What are "keywords" in google search that grab the attention of that group? How do you fit those concepts into your Primary Point of Differentiation? Google analytics is a fairly simple program that provides a real-time and historic tracking report card on how effective your messaging is... **Don't half-ass this!**

Be a blogging machine

You need a blog that offers consistent, valuable, relevant content. Use photos, graphics and links to articles, websites and videos that support your content. Blogs are one of the most efficient tools to tell your story, and customer stories that uniquely enhance your brand. Blogging has become a nearly automatic search on websites and search engines LOVE blogs! Google will reward you for great, consistent content by pushing your blog toward the top of their search pages. Websites with effective blogs get better than 50% more traffic than those who don't. Websites with blogs get twice as many inbound links than those who don't. Blogs attract more new visits and shared content than anything else on your website. Your blog is the heartbeat of your website!

Hubspot.com recently conducted a major survey of consumers age 18-54 that concluded that almost evenly across the entire, broad demo, those surveyed prefer **video content**. You need a consistent presence on You tube! Turn your blog into a "Vlog". Move towards video content for all social media posts. Use video testimonials as often as possible. You don't need overpriced video equipment to shoot effective video. Smartphones do just fine, and they are considered more "real". Not comfortable on camera? Some small businesses choose to narrate off-camera Power point presentations. Bottom line... Give consumers what they want... **Video!** You'll be amazed at the results compared to text-only blogs. **Don't half-ass this!**

Dickerson Orthodontics gets it!

Dickerson Orthodontics is a client of mine who uses video very effectively to deliver their message theme... "Orthodontics should be fun!" Dr. Todd Dickerson is universally recognized as a true leader in advancing new orthodontics procedures that lead to a quicker patient process from start to finish. Dickerson Orthodontics gets most patients through the braces process in half the time the other orthodontists do, and have fun throughout! Local consumers know them as the most fun, comfortable orthodontics choice in the valley. Even the mention of braces to most youngsters draws a look of horror and dismay. Dickerson Orthodontics doesn't. When you walk into one of the now 5 Dickerson locations you will likely encounter a lobby filled with mini beach balls, party favors, a digital camera on a tripod to take goofy family photos... The real differentiator is Dr. Dickerson's wild pants! He wears some really ridiculous golf pants every day! He has a closet with nearly 30 pairs of goofy pants. We created a video campaign for Facebook and You tube that features Dr. Dickerson reminding viewers that they'll get the best results in half the time. The video closes with a slow motion shot of Dr. Dickerson's pants walking away from the camera down the hall from his office to the exam room with the theme from "Chariots of fire" playing in the background. Dickerson Orthodontics understands their messaging is all about the unique customer experience, not boring facts about their business that people tune-out. Dickerson is now a **"Category of ONE"** based on the totally unique, fun atmosphere and patient experience they have built in the market. It's just the way they operate. No patient heads to the "procedure chair" without a smile on their face. It is also very clear that EVERYONE on the team absolutely loves their job! Oh, I almost forgot to mention that every Dickerson Orthodontics location has a soft ice cream machine to enjoy at the end of your appointment... Who doesn't love soft ice cream? Dickerson Orthodontics makes an emotional connection. **Don't half-ass this!**

Drop and give me 20!

For my money there's nothing more inspiring than a self-made success story with a "rags to riches" story behind it...

Erik Bryan was a marine and decorated war hero in Somalia & Desert storm. When he came home he decided to learn the heating & air conditioning business from the ground up. He did some apprentice work for a while, then in 1998 he launched in Precision Air & Heating with just a truck, a phone book and a bad-ass attitude! Today Precision Air & Heating is the largest HVAC company in

Arizona. Precision is also the highest rated. Erik turned his small business into a **Category of ONE** by using "Military influenced management" from day one. The first time I witnessed this firsthand was when I attended one of his weekly 7am Tech meetings. I have NEVER seen someone command a room like Erik. His no BS style, with a touch of humor now and then is truly unique. The entire room of easily distracted, blue collar technicians is glued to every word he says. He never has to repeat himself. How many bosses can say that? Erik is a supreme motivator as well. His team knows he has been on the front lines of war and isn't afraid to join them today. But Erik has a quality that too many managers lack these days... he's a great **listener!** He communicates with, not AT his team in group and individual settings. He personally demonstrates new techniques and equipment for his technicians to keep them modernized at all times. But Erik demands accountability! No unnecessary upselling customers, which in itself is unique to the industry. His team is bonused based on customer reviews. Erik handles every customer issue personally. Erik is always accessible. Erik demands every technician wash their truck every morning before they head out for the day. Erik demands proper hygiene. Erik demands that no technician leave a customer's property until they have clearly explained and educated the customer the reason for every service they provide and answer every question or concern on the spot. The result is a team that has earned great personal and professional pride. Precision Air & Heating also boasts the longest average tenure for technicians in the state of Arizona. Erik recruits only the best values and the best self-motivated technicians. Precision's motto is "People before Profits", and they practice it every day. Erik is a master technician himself and that builds great trust with his team, much like a group of marines respect their commander. Erik maintains a perspective backed by experience. He has established a unique income structure that allows every technician the opportunity to make a very good living (several make 6 figures).

Erik has also recently launched New A/C UNIT.com. The first online direct to consumer site in the HVAC industry. Newacunit.com allows customers to shop for the unit they want online, with the assistance of detailed breakdowns of every unit to educate customers to make the most efficient decision. Erik also applies Military influenced management with newacunit.com. We're currently in the process of developing a video e-book called "Military influenced management... works!" Typical Erik, it will include helpful tips for anyone in the HVAC industry to share. Erik is a giver. Obviously newacunit.com has exploded in the e-commerce world. Erik Bryan's story is a perfect example of how to turn your small business into a **Category of ONE!**

The anti-lawyer Lawyer!

I knew the minute I meant Byron Browne that he would be the IDEAL client to work with! He greeted me in his office at 10 am on a Tuesday in a tank top, flip-flops, shorts, and a variety of tattoos. He also had a great sense of humor and upbeat personality. That certainly breaks any high-browed, stuffy stereotypes ordinary lawyers live with. Byron was already a physical presence **Category of ONE!** We were able to move directly to working on messaging that captivates, motivates and activate his target consumer group.

Byron is a personal injury attorney. His target consumer group is people who have been in an accident and monetary damages are a big part of finalizing their case. So, we sat down and discussed the primary problems we needed to solve for a majority of consumers. Turns out the length of time it takes to get a monetary settlement is problem #1. They also don't want a paralegal from a big firm handling their case. Byron personally handles EVERY case he takes on. It only takes about 5 minutes for a new client to realize they are dealing with someone very unique. He dresses in a suit in court but that's the only place he puts his super casual outfits aside. Byron only uses paralegals to do research work and material prep. Byron handles all communication with his clients, the court and the insurance companies himself.

Browne law group ran a series of No BS "anti-lawyer Lawyer" videos on digital and social media sites to great success! They were highly entertaining and used visuals like his suit sleeves magically ripped off his arms while he is talking to proudly show his tattoos and tank top. His Primary Point of Differentiation was his appearance, attitude and client experience. He looks rough and tuff, but he's a very smart teddy bear. In Phoenix you can't drive 3 blocks without seeing a personal Injury lawyer billboard that all say the same thing! They all claim they can get you a check faster than the other guys. Wow, that's original?! Byron also has a unique strategy for getting in front of his potential target consumer group... he has a presence at several civic events, huge pet events and joined one of the largest motorcycle clubs in Arizona. Byron knows that most motorcycle accident cases don't find the motorcycle operator at fault. Motorcycle accidents unfortunately also have the most traffic related, consistent serious injuries with long healing processes. Now, a majority of motorcycle clubs **SEEK HIM OUT** for help, and he delivers. By the way, most judges love him for his personality, no BS process and efficiency. That's how he delivers monetary awards faster. There's never any "fake news" in his approach. Browne law group is truly a **Category of ONE!**

Customer retention tool

Dickerson Orthodontics, Precision Air & Heating and Browne law group are proof that effective Content Marketing can also improve customer retention. Content marketing is about building trust and credibility BEFORE you spend valuable resources on advertising. You'll notice that content marketing requires very little, if any, monetary resources. The only resource Content Marketing really demands is your time, focus and consistency. How's that for efficient, affordable and effective? If you keep consumers informed on new products, concepts or services, they will become loyal to you and your small business. Everyone likes to feel like they are "ahead of the curve" on industries they do business with. Show them that every particular customer benefit means just as much to your business as it does to them. Give them information like this constantly. Remember, Content Marketing has no finish line, but does have customer attrition if executed poorly. B2B marketers, get a feel for what kind of content is the most popular with your target business clients on Linkedin.com through their Linked in trending tool. Like google analytics, it too is easy to learn. Content marketing is a great method of building repeat visitors to your website, social media and bottom line, but it requires spending quality time on consumer research to find keywords that trigger their activation. **Don't half-ass this!**

Humor is a great activator!

Humor is the most effective way to present your content, but only if it's truly humorous and unoffensive. The tough part of this strategy is that humor is completely subjective. If you like to include jokes into your presentation, make sure you tailor them to the room you're speaking to. Most jokes aren't universally accepted, on purpose. You have to be confident that at least a vast majority of those who choose to click on your content think it's humorous, unless you actually want a "bad boy" reputation that you hope may disrupt your industry. Humor also tends to create a comfortable feeling when consumers determine who to do business with. I quote the great Dan Kennedy in his book "Make 'em laugh and take their money", "people buy more and buy more happily when in good humor". Just make sure the buying experience matches the tone of your content. The business killer that often gets ignored is when potential customers make a comment or give feedback like… "Wow, this place seems a lot different than their You tube videos seem to show. Very disappointing". Keep the core personality of your small business consistent throughout the buying process. NEVER underwhelm or disappoint potential customers by violating the perception your messaging, marketing and advertising presents, regardless of the media platform! **This is a game changer… in the wrong direction**. If your marketing message is truly unique, the buying experience needs to match it. Pleasantly surprise them. Becoming a **"Category of ONE"** is about the sum of all the parts of the customer's experience. I remind you yet again that your marketing message is NOT about you or your business. It's about filtering every single marketing message element through the mindset of potential customers. **Don't half-ass this!**

Storytelling

Storytelling is by far the most effective strategy for humorous or emotional content. The more real and believable it is, the more humorous it is. Most stand-up comics use storytelling to deliver their jokes on just about anything through building anticipation of the punchline. Do what the pros do. Hire humorous content writers to "humor up" your standard content if need be. You can find them all over google search. Build consumer anticipation for your content and watch your content sharing and revenue explode! **Don't half-ass this!**

Characters can make a real difference!

Creating a character representing your business is perhaps the best kept secret to compelling Content Marketing. One of my greatest client success stories was an extended campaign for Jay Lee Auto in Portland. In our initial creative meeting with Jay, we learned that he wanted a totally unique campaign that didn't look, feel or sound like EVERY other auto dealer campaign. He wanted a humorous character that would intrigue customers and give them a unique reason to come to the dealership. My first thought was… this needs to be a **contrarian** campaign that uses ridiculous humor to drive home the unique buying experience customers will enjoy at Jay Lee Auto. I created a character named "Cecil". Cecil is Jay Lee's black sheep nephew who screws up everything he touches. Cecil had a voice that pronounced every "s" sound with that sloppy, back of the mouth sound that is so annoying. Cecil became so popular that customers came into the dealership wanting to meet Cecil! This serial campaign had a new episode every 2 weeks and lasted over 2 years, which is a multiple of lifetimes for typical campaigns. Jay Lee Auto became widely known as the "Cecil dealership". We created posters of the mess Cecil would leave behind in every department and hung them side by side in the showroom. No visual of Cecil ever appeared. Just the "theater of the mind" that allowed customers to picture what Cecil looked like in their own minds. Jay Lee auto has put themselves into a **"Category of ONE!"**

Charlie Fm

In 2006 the President of Entercom Communications and VP of Programming came to Portland to discuss launching a brand new radio format. They had a very vague idea of what they were looking for, but it had to be completely unique. I'll never forget the end of that meeting when the corporate guys said to me... "Dan, you've got a blank canvas... go paint it!" I've never felt so anxious to give birth to something brand new that I started conceptualizing that night. What could I create that would take the market by storm and create organic, word of mouth growth before we spent a dime on advertising? Charlie Fm became one of the pioneers of the "Adult Hits" format. We played every hit song from 1967-2006 in complete random order. Every song-to-song transition was an absolute train wreck, on purpose. Charlie would play Motley Crue's "Girls, Girls, Girls" into "Rhinestone Cowboy". There were no live dj's, but there were several fictitious characters including Charlie's mom, a hippie named Randy, Leon Freon's "word of the day", Davis Wellington III was our 6 year old General Manager... These characters would show up on the air in 10 second snippets between songs several times an hour. We had a comment line that listeners would call and leave messages for the characters and actually referred to them by name. Within 3 months Charlie-Fm became the dominant #1 station in virtually every adult demo in Portland. It was initially somewhat polarizing with advertisers, but not for long. Then just a few months later the heaven's opened up and the revenue started flowing in. We were sold out of advertising inventory for 18 months! We built a website that visitors could click on any character to hear every snippet on demand. **We didn't half-ass this!**

Webinars!

Webinars are very effective presenting you and your small business as a tangible, information source viewers feel a real connection to. The best webinars are an online video follow up to your most effective blogs, social media posts or book. People always want more content about things that are interesting, educational and matter to them. Webinars are a terrific tool to build credibility and "go-to expert" perceptions. Effective webinars include sharp on-screen graphics, infographics, tables, surveys and any other visual that supports your webinar content. You'll need to practice your delivery and execution. You need to be so comfortable delivering your content that viewers feel like you're having a conversation with them vs. just reading a script. Conversational presentation leads to that "go-to expert" status with viewers. Adobe, Final cut and Wondershare have very simple video editing programs even I can grasp in minutes. If you happen to be camera shy or just not very good on video, use someone from your office, a local celebrity or hire a professional speaker to deliver your webinar. I've seen some very effective webinars that were hosted by team members on the frontline of the business. They are likely to deliver your content with more, genuine emotion. Give them the freedom to include a little ad-libbing when they have something personal to share. Webinar viewers appreciate hearing from the support team. They feel like they're going "behind the curtain" of your business and it builds deeper credibility. More good news, there's no real time limit on webinars as long as it's edited properly and moves the conversation forward.

One strategy that almost never fails is webinar and social media content around a debate. This where I often take a contrarian stance on an emotional issue solely to activate the masses. Nothing sparks response and engagement more than a controversial stance on an issue the majority are likely passionate about on both sides. Be an instigator (it's fun) and reap the participation rewards from consumers. I've seen social media threads go on for weeks around a webinar on an emotional issue that instigates real debate. Just make sure you have filters on offensive language or threats of any kind. You need to be prepared to have eyes on every post during debate topics. The key is to present an inviting, inclusive platform that doesn't violate common sense decency. Controversial comments are great! Engagement is awesome! Offensive comments only damage your product or service. You certainly don't want truly offensive content shared across social media. **Don't half-ass this!**

Attack yourself!

Yup, at least twice a year, you need to spend some serious time attacking yourself! Tear apart every component of your business and find any vulnerability. Unless you're in some kind of denial, you'll always find some areas of vulnerability. I always require at least 3 vulnerabilities to find solutions for every time we attack ourselves. Keep in mind, there are no sacred cows when attacking your business. Attack each component and find a solution before moving on to the next component. To truly be a **"Category of ONE"**, you need to be honest and accountable to yourself. No one can attack you better than you! This exercise always builds energy and motivation as a result. It feels good to know you've found solutions internally, including even the smallest opportunities to improve your business. Present those challenges as a positive motivator to your team. With inclusion comes buy-in. Give your team a sense of ownership with every vulnerability solution. Let them know how each solution is opportunity for them, not a directive. **Don't half-ass this!**

Never rely on a single revenue stream!

Operating a small business is a huge undertaking. You need to protect it. Relying on a single revenue stream is the most vulnerable thing you can do. You open yourself up to competitor attacks and unexpected changes to your industry that can bring you down in a heartbeat. You can have a clear messaging focus on a single revenue stream, but you need at least one secondary revenue source to protect against unexpected circumstances. Protecting your assets can be anything from building a subscription model for newsletters, to offering special online only specials, to public speaking, to publishing a book for your business. This strategy also has the tendency to grow fringe customers into loyal customers. Differentiation is the key to every revenue stream you structure. This is where a solid Content Marketing strategy does it's best work for you. Use your social media to post content to drive all revenue streams. Testimonials, especially video testimonials are another great tool for secondary revenue streams. Don't be a copycat with any revenue stream. Put your business' core personality into every revenue stream to differentiate your business. You can be a **"Category of ONE"** with how you present and message your revenue streams. **Don't half-ass this!**

Wanna be a leader? ACT like one!

Domination is earned, not granted. Captivation, motivation and activation are results of your messaging. Perceptual leadership from consumers comes more from peer to peer sharing than ANY advertising campaign. Keep that fact in mind.

Leaders are omnipresence. They consistently deliver relevant information across multiple media platforms. They know where and when their potential customers are likely on one of your social platforms. They understand that nothing leads to long-term revenue growth more than content that matters to your target consumers. Leaders put content delivery at the top of their strategic plan. Leaders seize every opportunity to positively impact their target consumer market. Leaders understand strong content delivery on social media is **FREE**! You won't be bothered by pushy media reps. To ignore this platform is simply lazy. Leaders understand consumers begin to count on us to educate them. This is where true trust and credibility are built. Consumers understand you don't have to educate them, you choose to. You're a giver! That matters to consumers. Leaders aren't necessarily great writers, they are CONSISTENT content providers. They speak the language of their consumers, not inside buzz terms. Leaders are constantly engaging their consumers, inviting feedback and responding.

To be completely honest, today's small businesses need to ultimately have someone fully dedicated to consumer engagement across all media platforms to maximize growth. YOU need to keep control of the content messaging themes yourself, but a team member can be in charge of executing it. Ideally, it's adding a fulltime position to your team. Outsourcing can be a temporary option, but you'll find that one of the most important recruitments you'll do is for your **content provider specialist**. Put that position near the top of your company flow chart! This is a true differentiator your competitors will likely be caught off guard by. Pounce on this opportunity as soon as possible! If you truly want to be a leader, act like one! **Don't half-ass this!**

Create a Video Sales Letter!

Direct mailer Sales Letters are great, when done remarkably. Remember video is by far the preferred source for making real connections with consumers! You'll find all the evidence you need at www.hubspot.com. Video makes you more tangible and believable, which should equate to trust and credibility. You've got to give yourself every advantage you can. You can do both, direct mail and video messaging. Use the video Sales Letter initially. Then follow up with the direct mailer Sales Letter as phase 2.

You don't need to spend a pile of cash on a slick, professional video shoot. Your smart phone is another HD video source these days. The key is to shoot the video in your workspace as though you're simply pausing to have a conversation with viewers. Some clients have gone the "outrageous" route with their setting and background. I caution you if you're thinking of doing the same, you choose a setting that matches your own AND business core personality. Don't ever send out anything that could confuse or cause the "huh?" factor from viewers.

Built-in testimonials are extremely effective with any Sales Letter, but especially video Sales Letters. They are instantly believable and trusted by viewers. Just make sure the customers you use have genuine personality and aren't afraid to show it in text or video.

Make sure you put your Sales Video Letter on every relevant social, digital and online you use. Obviously, You tube and your website are automatic platforms to use. There's no reason to keep your unique marketing message a secret. I would also suggest putting your Video Sales Letter on a thumb drive to include with your direct mailers. Make sure you have a checklist of all marketing and advertising platforms. **Don't half-ass this!**

Dan Kennedy is a GENIOUS!

I would be absolutely remiss if I didn't give credit to the man who inspired me to take the path I've chosen after a 27-year career in Creative Media management. Dan Kennedy is a Master Copywriter who commands 6 figures for a single project. How? He's earned it! He's actually underpaid! He's the absolute BEST in the business! He charges around $19,000 per day for his consulting services and you have to go to HIM! However, Dan is probably best known for authoring his best-selling series called "No BS Marketing". For my money, this series of books is the best marketing training material on the planet! It's unbelievably practical and easy to implement. His hundreds of successful examples of everything from unique direct response messaging to eye-catching Sales Letters to remarkably creative direct mailer packaging options will keep you coming back to his content for every advertising campaign. My single favorite book Dan wrote with Bill Glazer is called **"Outrageous Advertising"**. Just trust me on this, you need to order this book TODAY! Full disclosure, I have never met Dan Kennedy. He has no idea who I am. That's ok, his content is worth sharing with every small business owner out there. Get his books. Share them with everyone on your team. It will galvanize your whole team and serve as an evergreen source when you run into "writer's block" or searching for great brainstorming material. Dan lays everything out for your unique advertising to work. You just need to roll up your sleeves and practice inserting your specific messaging. Yes, practice. It's very rare to have great success with your initial campaign. That's why we encourage you to launch every campaign in 3 phases. Tackle it like an athlete. You can't practice too much. For some management folks it may sound ironic, but practicing is actually a great use of your team's time. It's also a great way to maintain that outside/in posture that consumers recognize and respond to. **Don't half-ass this!**

Take this…

If there's anything you grasp from this book, I hope it's this…

Successful advertising, no matter how big or small your budget, is about PREPARING to advertise. It's about removing as much risk as possible BEFORE you spend another dime on advertising.

Small business success is not just about providing products or services as much as it is about providing SOLUTIONS!

I personally thank you for giving me far more of your attention than I deserve. I would love to hear from you! Contact me at dan@killermessaging.com and you have my word I will respond. Challenge me. Call me out on anything in this book. This book is not gospel, it's about opinion and perspective influenced by experience. I never stop learning, and you are the best teacher through your stories and challenges. The greatest feeling in the world is knowing you've made a positive difference. It's a mutual benefit. The only metric that truly matters when it comes to advertising is **RETURN ON INVESTMENT!** Good luck and...

Don't half-ass this!

www.ingramcontent.com/pod-product-compliance
Lightning Source LLC
Chambersburg PA
CBHW031546210526
45464CB00003B/1176